Fashion
COLORING BOOK
VOLUME ONE

april heather
ART ♥ ILLUSTRATION

www.AprilHeatherArt.com

I HAVE A QUESTION.

What happens when you make time for something you love to do? Just a little time. Something that brings you joy, calm, peace. What if you take that thing - whatever it may be - and you share it with others? What happens then? These are the questions I was asking myself last winter.

Winter is tough for me - this native Texan gets pretty blue under dark and moody Pennsylvania skies come January. Although I was busy with the day to day running of my Etsy shops, meeting the demands of being a mom to two delightful teenage girls, and managing the home, meals, life...I realized I wasn't drawing or painting everyday. Life had just gotten too busy.

I decided, for the sake of my own mental health, that I needed to carve out an hour a day to do what I absolutely love: create art. Not art for a purpose, just art I love. To illustrate what delighted me each and every day. My thinking was that if I made the time for this thing I love, I'd be better equipped to deal with the ups and downs of the rest of my life. Seems logical, right?

So I challenged myself to a personal project of doing 100 days of illustrations and my focus would be fashion. *I thought "In 100 days it will be warmer! It will be spring!"* I wasn't sure what kind of fashion to focus on or maybe just mix it up; runway, red carpet, historic fashion, or just everyday streetwear. I titled it "100 Days of Fashion" adding a hashtag to my posts to keep myself accountable and focused.

For inspiration I started bookmarking looks I loved from Instagram's many fashion bloggers and I pinned cool outfits in a Pinterest board entitled "figure poses." I sketched anytime I had a few minutes, carrying around a sketchpad everywhere I went. And then I started sharing my illustrations on Instagram and Facebook.

It was such a fun project, but it wasn't easy. In fact some days were a struggle - no doubt about it. I had days that I felt I could draw anything, and other days everything I drew or painted ended up in crumpled ball on the floor.

As time passed I realized my favorite things to illustrate are everyday women. Everyday women who are - one day at a time - changing modern beauty standards. They are changing how beauty is defined by just being themselves and doing what they love - and they have truly inspired me. I learned so much more than just painting skills during my 100 day project!

So, to answer my question: *What happens when you make time for something you love to do?* Turns out a little bit of magic happens. You connect with others in ways you may never have imagined. You grow in ways you didn't expect. Your days take on a new cadence and, in my experience, you get a little more giddy-up in your step. I'm super excited for each new illustration, for the experience of it - not just the results.

I hope you enjoy coloring the following pages of inspiring women and fashions. This is just the first 50 - more will be coming in 2018. It was an absolute joy to create each illustration and to share them with you.

Thank you, from the bottom of my heart.

xo♥, Heather

DRAWING + PAINTING EVERYDAY WOMEN EVERY DAY-ISH

"

I'm interested in seeing just
the girl on the street because
she is unlike any other.
I'm inspired by whatever it is
she might be wearing.

Anna Wintour

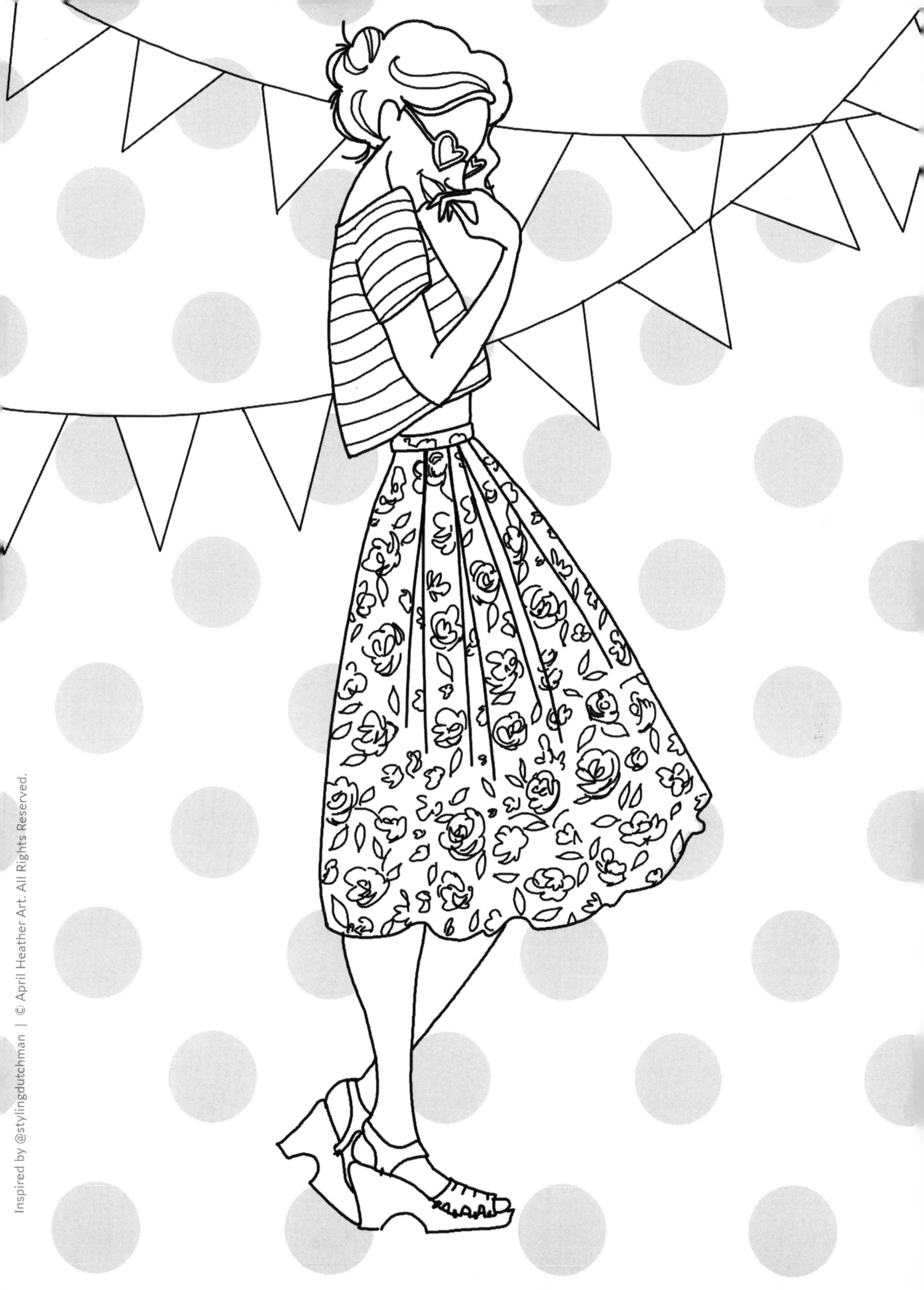

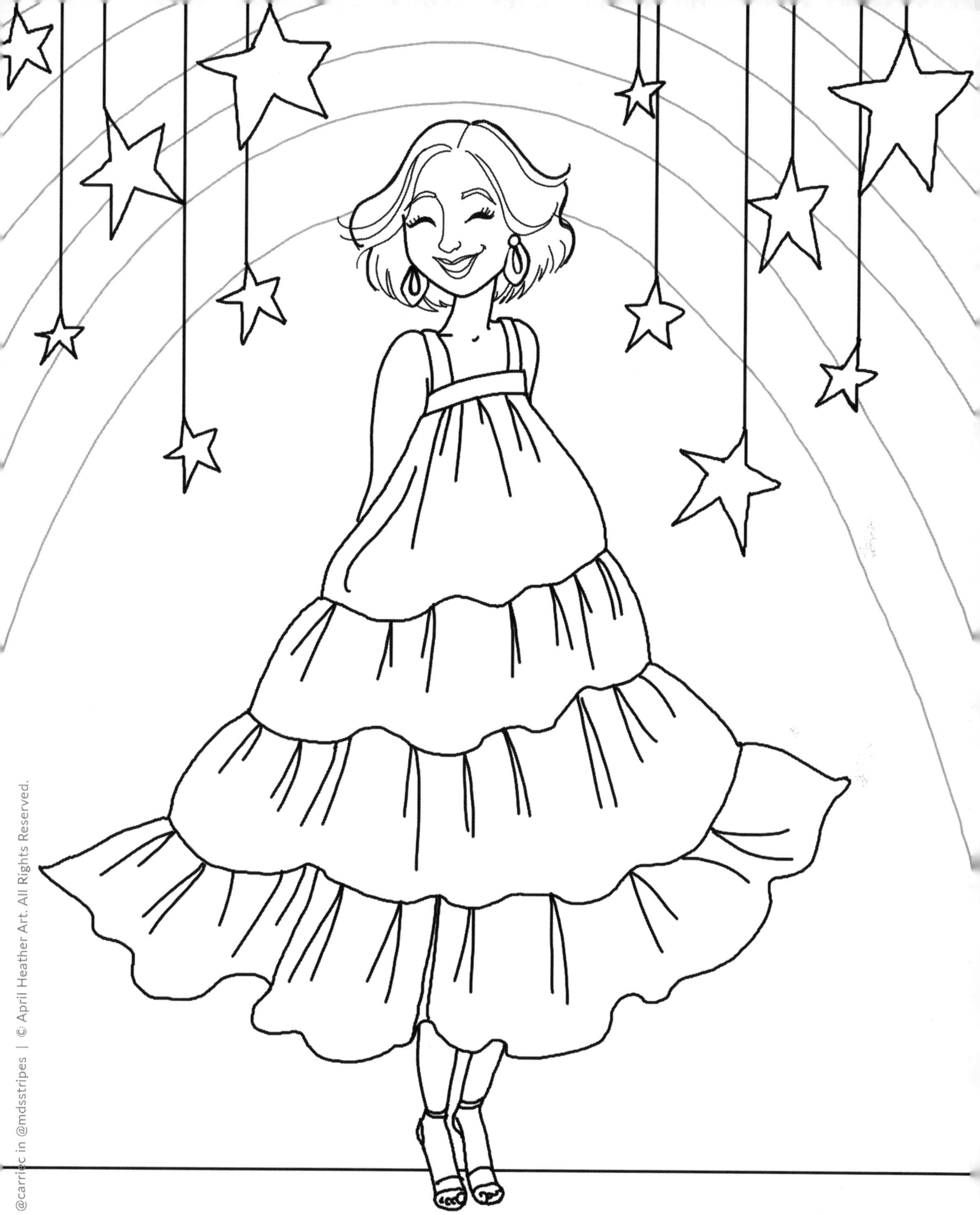

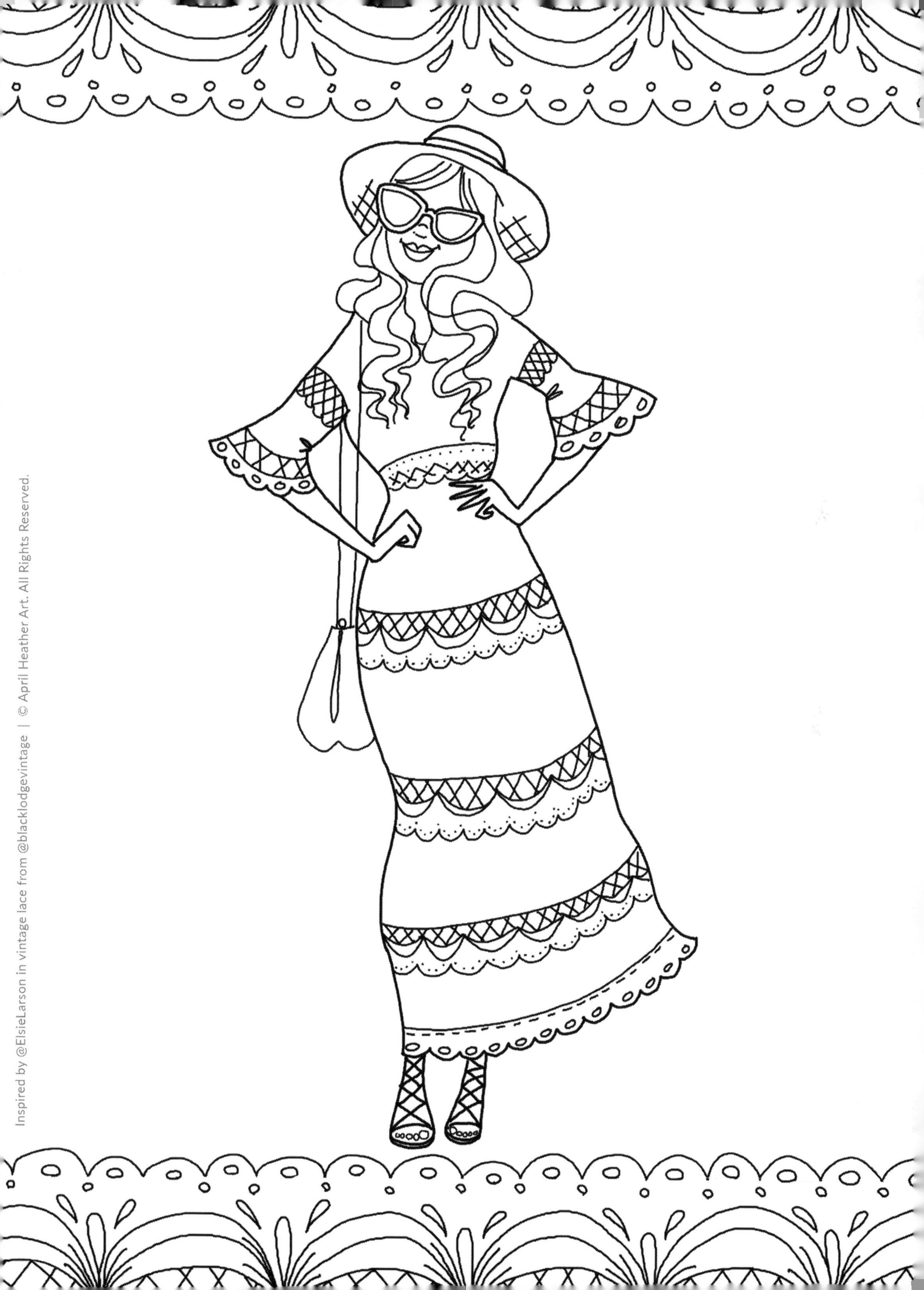

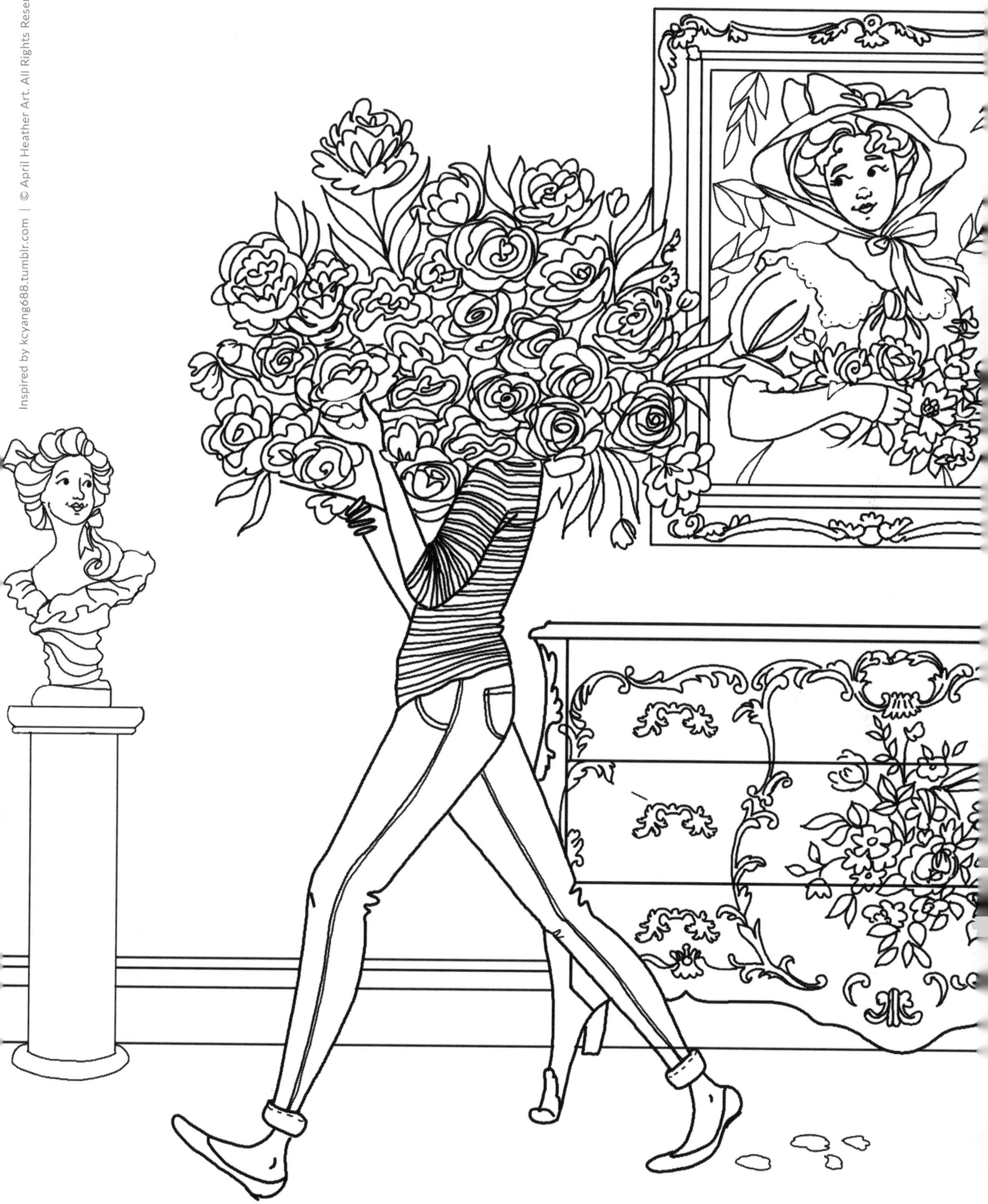

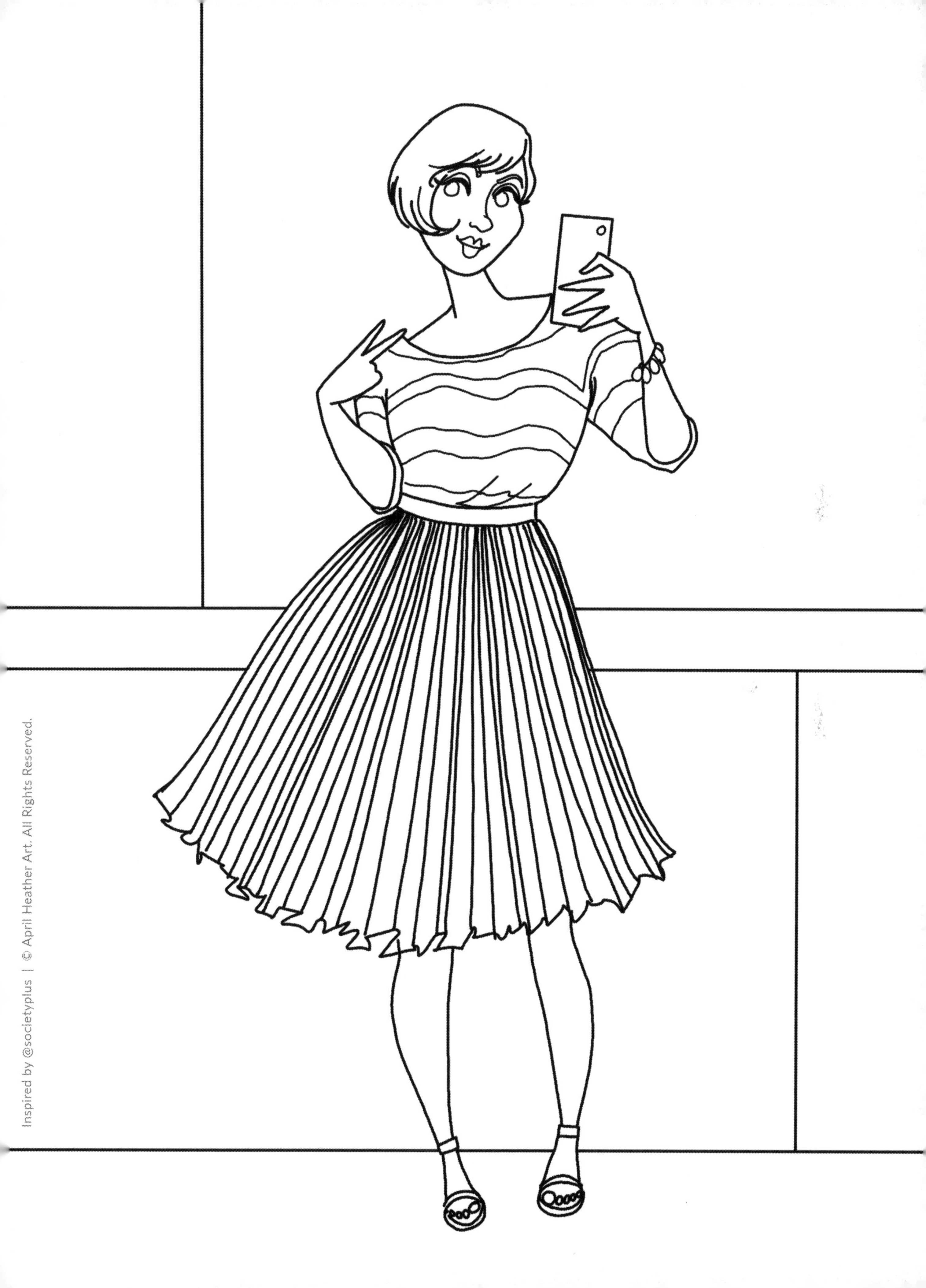

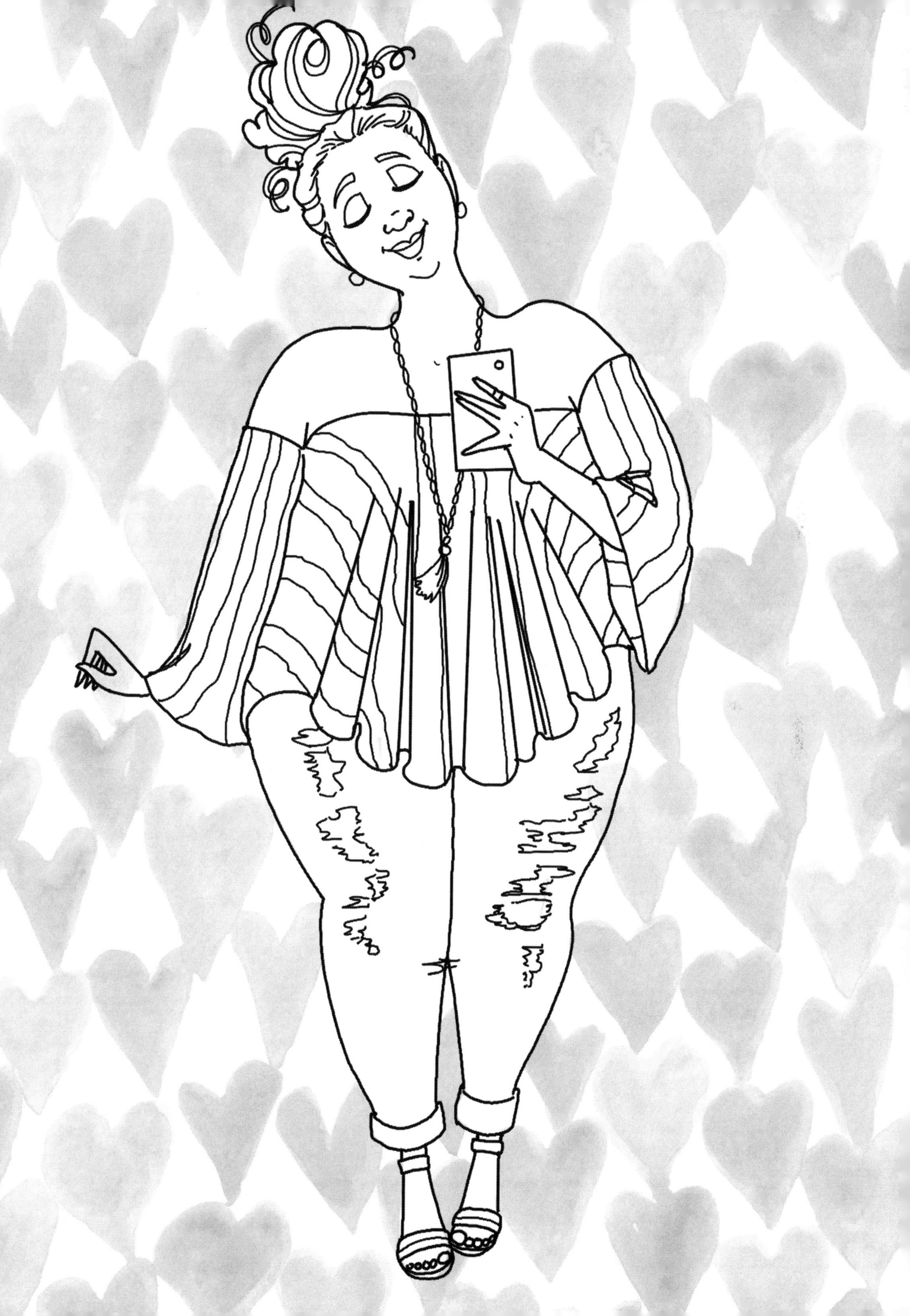

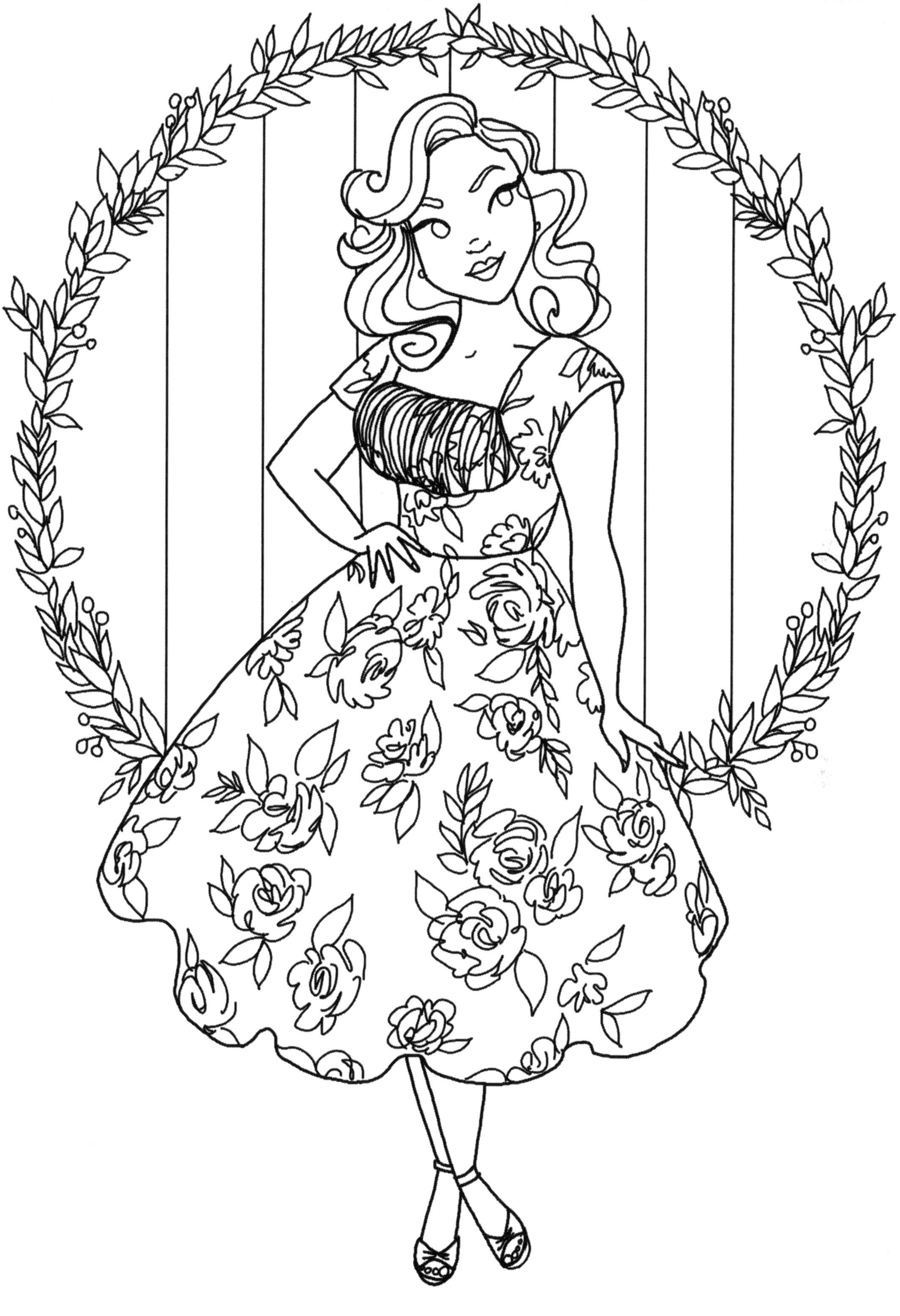

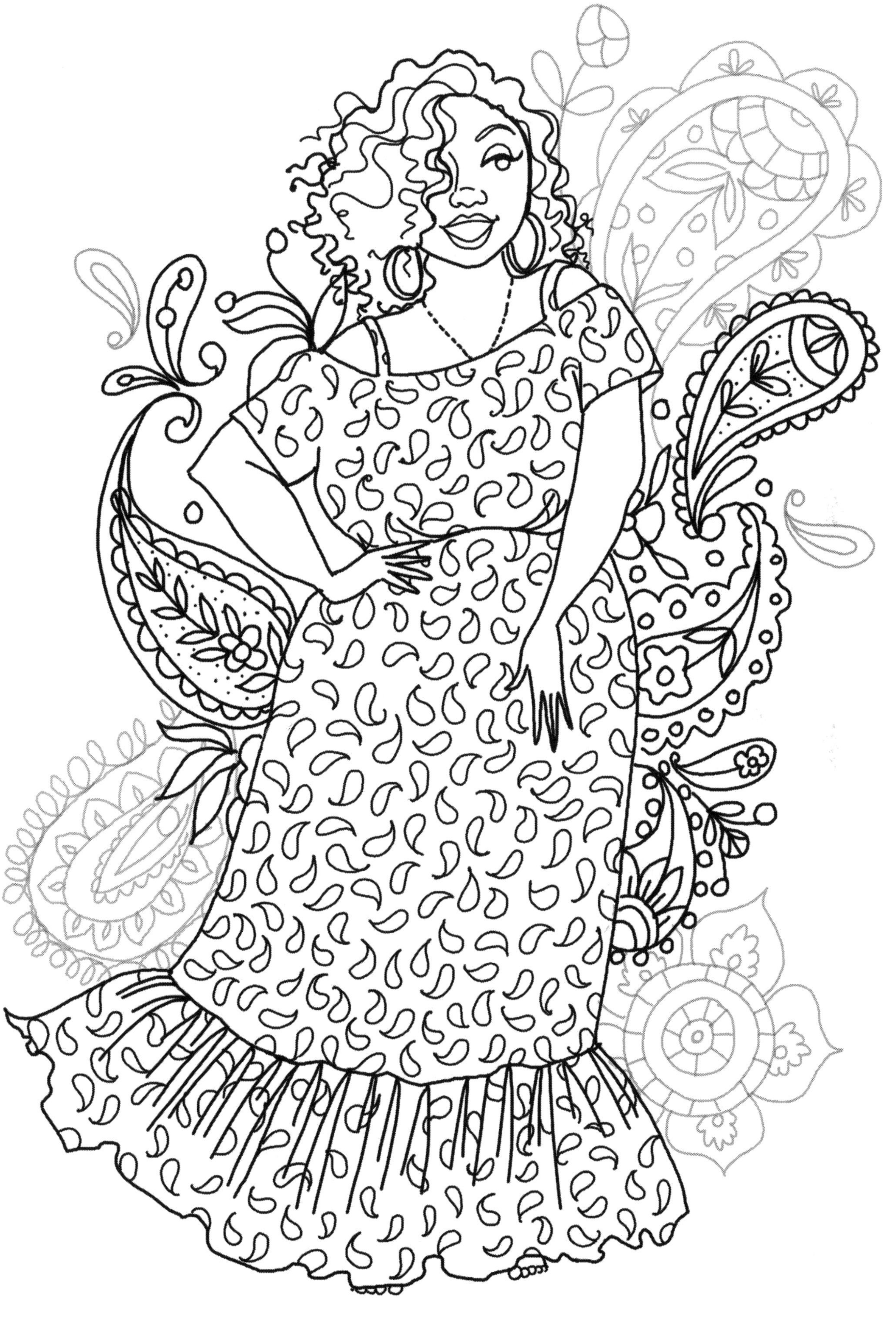

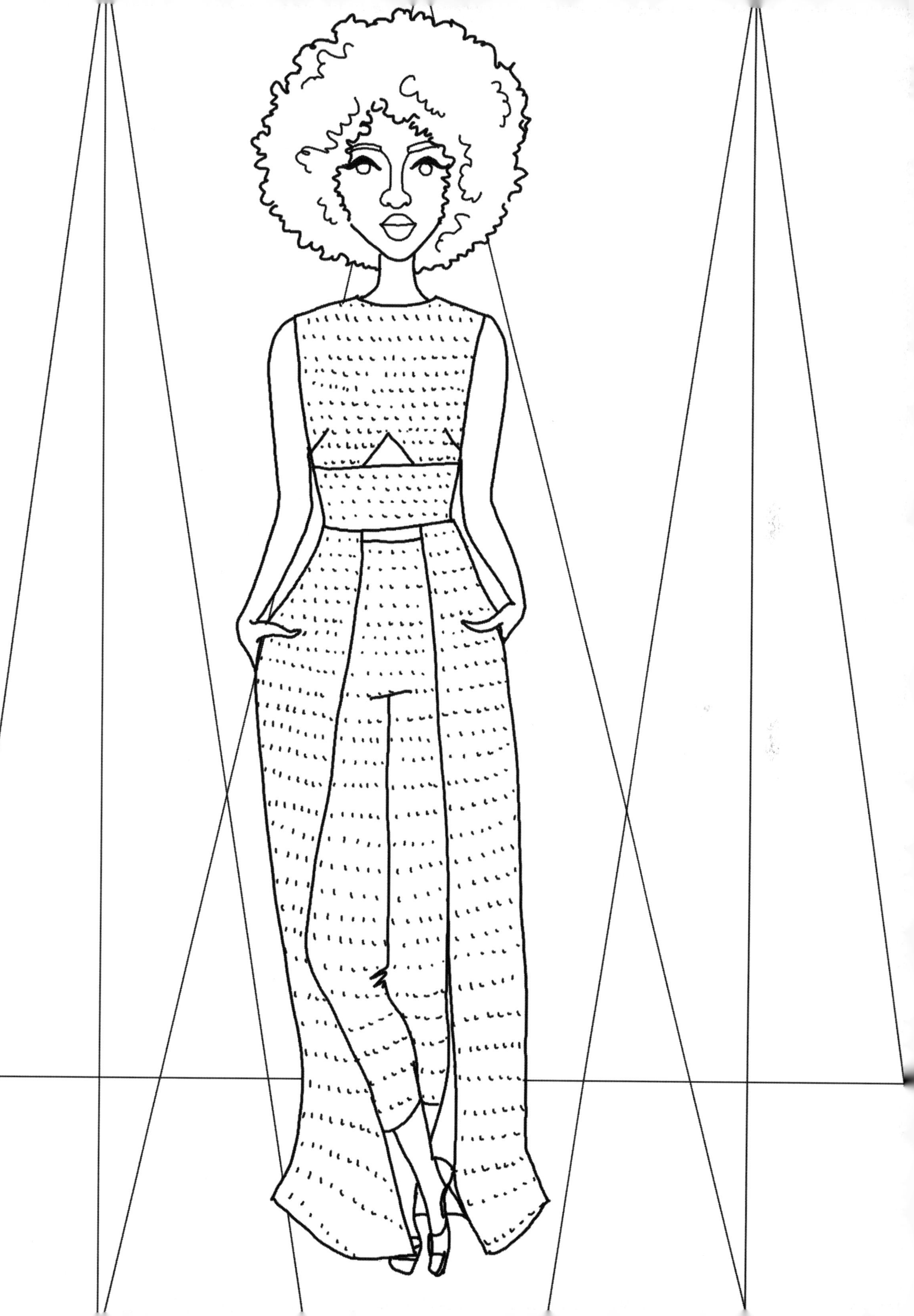

Sugar Coffee Tea

But first COFFEE

Inspired by @freepeople

FRENCH CAN

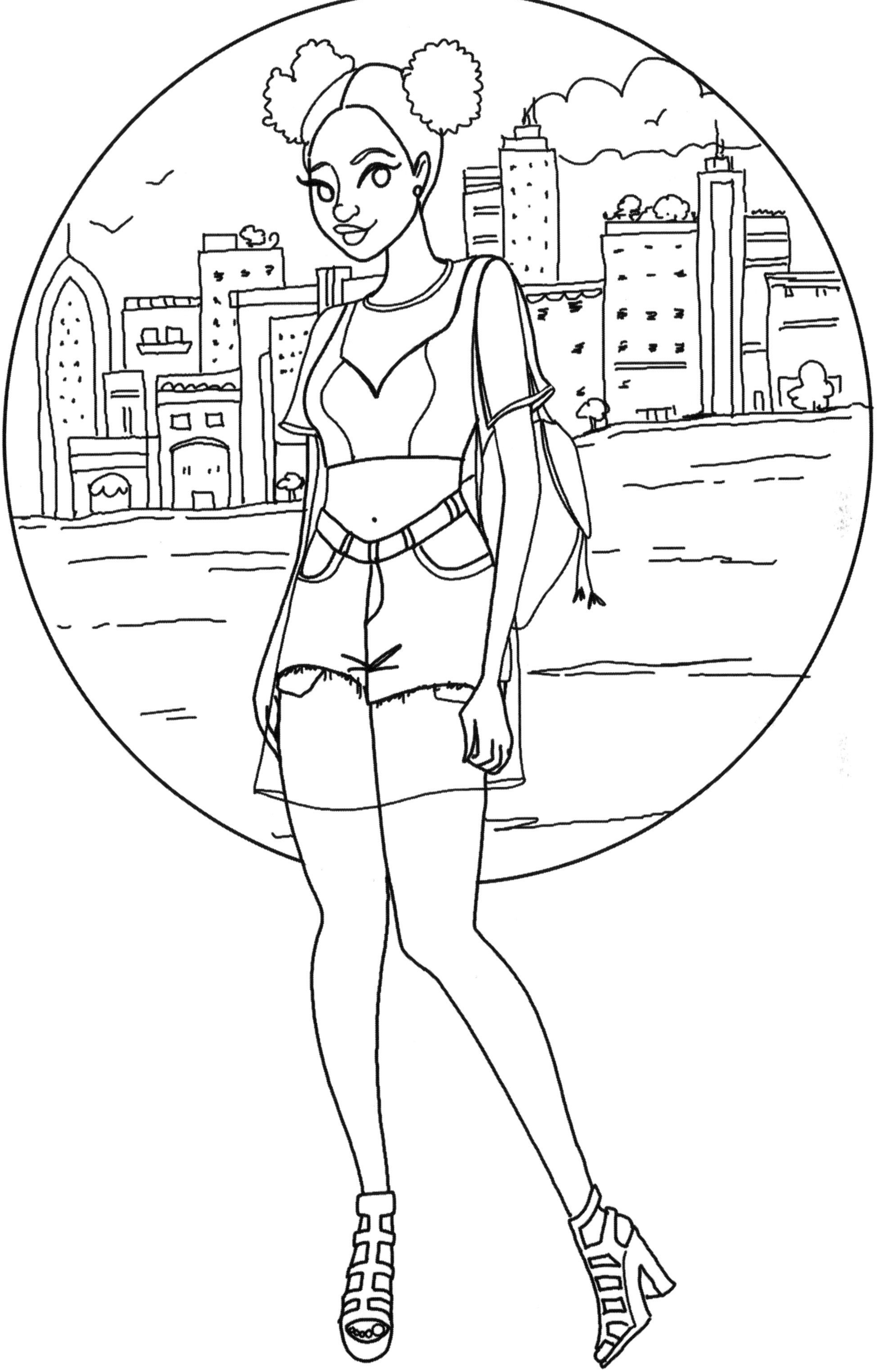

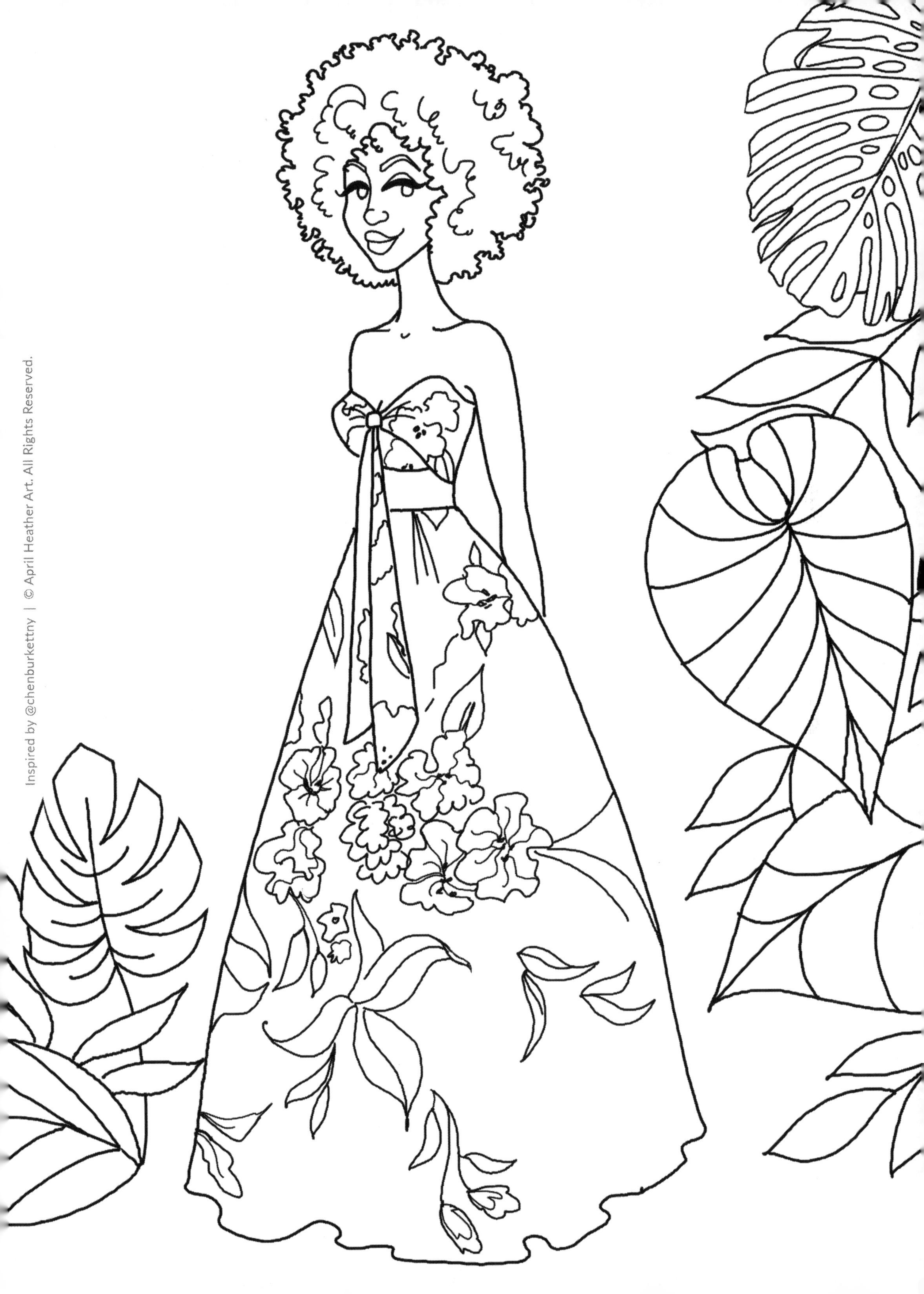

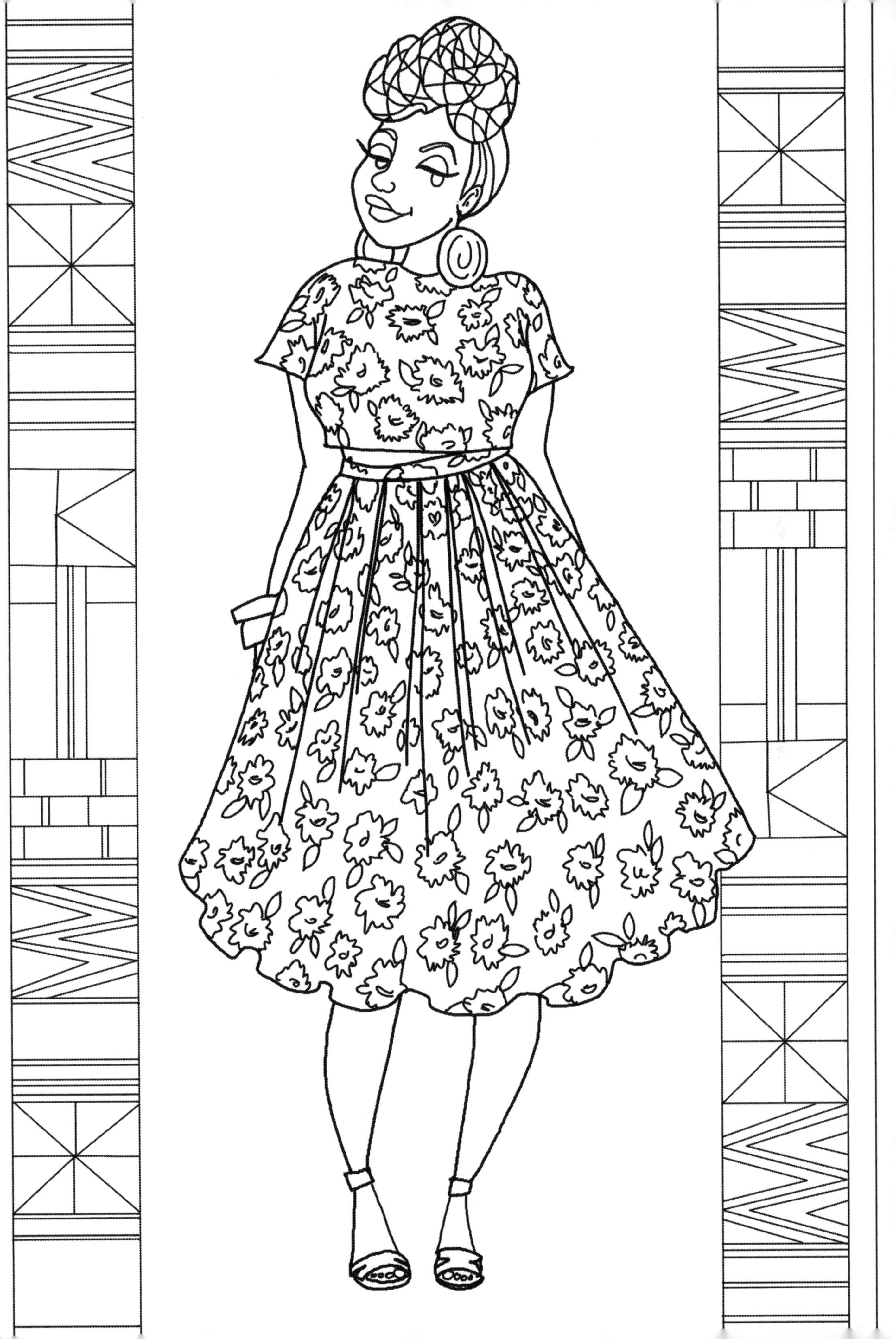

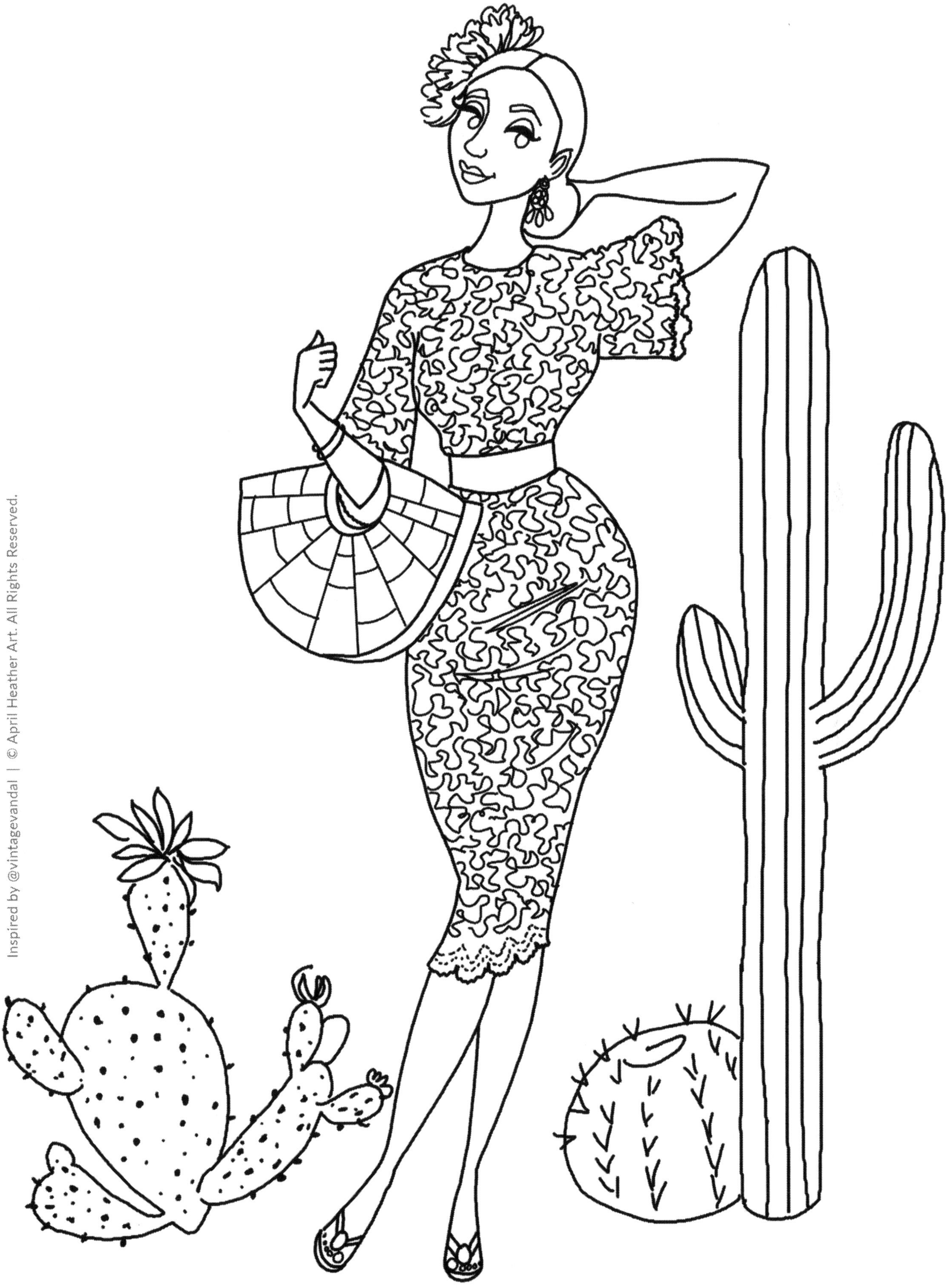

Let your love *Sparkle*

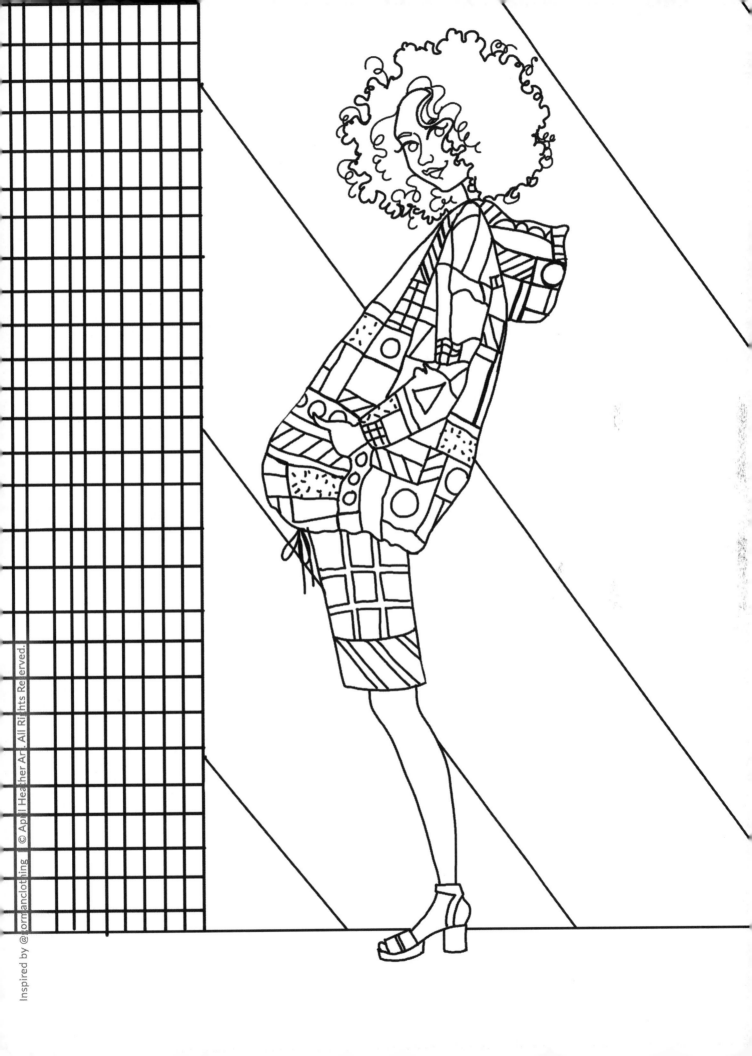

LOOKING *good*

Travel is the only thing you can buy that makes you Richer

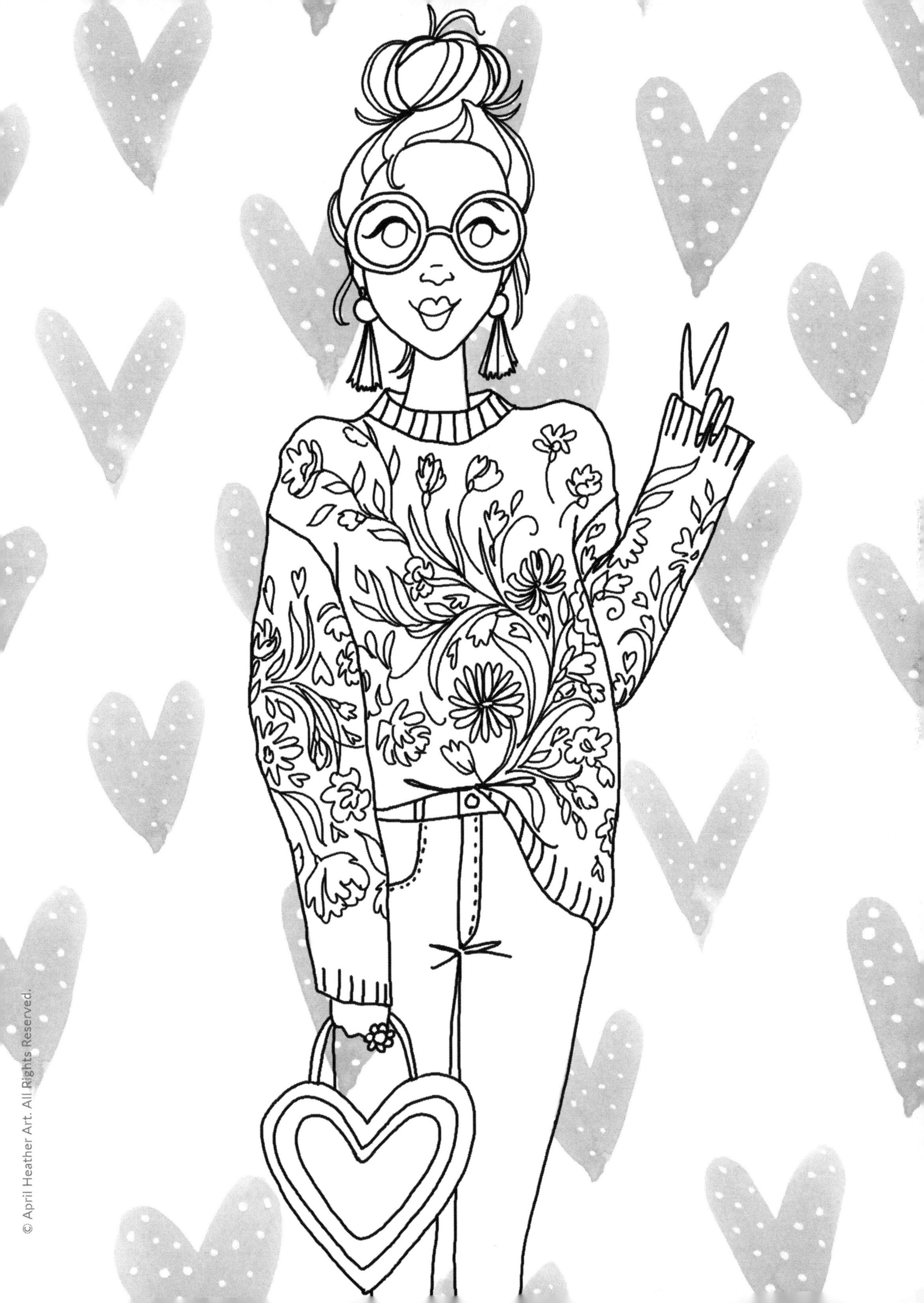

Made in the USA
San Bernardino, CA
17 April 2018